Animal Engineers

ANTHILLS

by Christopher Forest

FOCUS READERS

FOCUS READERS

www.focusreaders.com

Focus Readers is distributed by North Star Editions:
sales@northstareditions.com | 888-417-0195

Produced for Focus Readers by Red Line Editorial.

Photographs ©: AlexussK/Shutterstock Images, cover, 1; AG-PHOTOS/Shutterstock Images, 4–5; Eric Isselee/Shutterstock Images, 7; Pavel Krasensky/Shutterstock Images, 8–9; KlzTH/Shutterstock Images, 11; kurt_G/Shutterstock Images, 13; Gypsytwitcher/Shutterstock Images, 14–15; zatvornik/Shutterstock Images, 16–17; Bruce MacQueen/Shutterstock Images, 19, 29; Beneda Miroslav/Shutterstock Images, 20; Paul Clarke/Shutterstock Images, 22–23; baxys/Shutterstock Images, 24; Aldemar Bernal/Shutterstock Images, 26

ISBN
978-1-63517-856-2 (hardcover)
978-1-63517-957-6 (paperback)
978-1-64185-160-2 (ebook pdf)
978-1-64185-059-9 (hosted ebook)

Library of Congress Control Number: 2018931105

Printed in the United States of America
Mankato, MN
May, 2018

About the Author

Christopher Forest is a middle school teacher in Massachusetts. He has written stories, articles, and novels for readers of all ages. In his spare time, he enjoys watching sports, playing guitar, reading, and spending time outdoors.

TABLE OF CONTENTS

CHAPTER 1

AN UNDERGROUND HOME

A flurry of ants covers the ground. They are carrying small bits of food. The ants walk in a long line. They follow a path that has been worn through the grass.

Thousands of ants may live in one anthill.

Soon, the first ant reaches a pile of dirt. At the top is a hole. One by one, the ants go into the hole. Now they are inside the anthill. They crawl through a series of tunnels beneath the ground. These tunnels form the ants' home. It is known as an ant colony. The ants bring

FUN FACT

The largest ant colony in the world spreads from Italy to Spain. It stretches for 3,600 miles (5,790 km)!

 An ant carries a piece of an apple back to the colony.

the food into the tunnels. They will

store it underground.

CHAPTER 2

WORKING TOGETHER

There are three kinds of ants. They work together to build the anthill. Every anthill begins with a **queen**. She leaves an old anthill. Then she **mates** with a male. Next, she finds a safe place. She digs a hole.

A queen ant lays eggs inside the anthill.

This small **chamber** is the start of a new anthill.

The queen lays eggs. The eggs hatch into other ants. In time, male ants will mate with the queen. The female ants will become workers. They do not lay eggs. Instead, they make the colony bigger. Workers dig more tunnels. Some tunnels lead to

FUN FACT

A queen ant can live to be 30 years old.

 Worker ants dig near the entrance to an anthill.

the first chamber. Others connect

to new chambers.

A worker's strong **mandibles** can cut and carry objects. Workers use their mandibles to move pieces of dirt out of the colony. They carry the dirt up to a hole at the top. Then they leave the dirt outside this hole. As workers dig, the dirt piles up. In this way, the anthill grows. Some anthills are 1 inch (2.5 cm) high. Others can be 10 feet (3.0 m) tall.

A big anthill might **collapse**. To prevent this, ants mix pieces of leaves, sticks, or pine needles into

> An ant's mandibles can be different shapes depending on what kind of food it eats.

the dirt. This makes the anthill stronger. It also helps keep rain or snow out of the colony.

STAYING WARM AND DRY

Anthills are designed to protect ants from the weather. An anthill's **dome** shape helps it absorb the sun's heat. This keeps the ants warm. Ants might even add tiny holes in the dome. Opening the holes allows the ants to warm or cool the colony. But the holes can be sealed when it is rainy. Many ants add twigs, leaves, or small stones to their anthill as well. Some even add sap. These materials help make the anthill strong. They also help keep out wind and rain.

Mulga ants add needles from mulga trees to their anthills.

CHAPTER 3

INSIDE THE COLONY

The anthill is the entrance to the colony. Most of an ant colony is underground. Below the entrance are many tunnels. The tunnels connect the anthill's chambers. An ant colony has many chambers.

 Worker ants carry eggs to some chambers.

The chambers can be up to 15 feet (4.6 m) below the ground.

Ants use some chambers to store food. Other chambers hold eggs. Workers may use other chambers for resting. Some chambers hold aphids. Aphids are insects. They make a sweet substance called honeydew. Ants collect the

FUN FACT

Compared to ants, aphids are tiny. They are about the size of a pinhead.

An ant places a group of aphids on a leaf to feed them. Aphids make honeydew by eating plants.

honeydew. They use it as food. They feed it to baby ants.

Worker ants care for the young ants, which are still pale white.

Worker ants inside the colony have different jobs. Young ants begin working deep underground.

They care for the baby ants and dig tunnels or chambers for them. As the ants get older, they move to the middle levels of the hill. They extend the nest and store food. Older ants move to the top of the anthill. There, they gather food and protect the top part of the nest.

FUN FACT

Soldiers are a type of worker ant.
They protect the anthill from attackers.

CHAPTER 4

ANTHILL IMPACT

When ants build an anthill, they affect the area around them. Sometimes they cause harm. Ants may take **resources** and food from other animals. Or, they may build anthills in damp or rotting wood.

 Many anthills can be found in the Amazon rainforest.

Some ants build nests in trunks or logs.

Sometimes this wood is part of a building, such as a house. The ants' tunnels can make the building weaker.

But anthills can also be helpful. As ants dig tunnels, they move soil around. Some soil is brought up to the surface. Some soil is left in chambers inside the anthill. In this way, ants mix together soil from different layers. Material that was broken down deeper in the ground mixes with dirt near the top. This process adds **nutrients** to the soil. It helps plants grow. The mixing helps air and water flow through the soil, too.

There are more than 40 species of leafcutter ants. Many live in rainforests.

Ants also help keep the ground clear of dead leaves. Ants break apart leaves that fall to the ground. They use the leaf pieces to build their anthills.

Ants can even help other insects. For example, some grasshoppers lay eggs on anthills. The eggs hatch in the anthill's warm soil. Butterflies may rest on the anthills and **bask** in the sun. These are just a few reasons ants and their tunnels are an important part of nature.

FUN FACT

Sometimes two ant colonies fight. The ants swarm out of their anthills and attack one another.

FOCUS ON
ANTHILLS

Write your answers on a separate piece of paper.

1. Write a paragraph describing how ants build anthills.

2. Do you think anthills are helpful to the environment or harmful? Why?

3. Which type of ant lays eggs?
- **A.** soldier
- **B.** queen
- **C.** worker

4. What is the relationship between ants and aphids?
- **A.** Ants hide from the aphids, and the aphids eat the ants.
- **B.** Ants attack the aphids, and the aphids fight back against the ants.
- **C.** Ants protect the aphids, and the aphids produce food for the ants.

5. What does **connect** mean in this book?

*Some tunnels lead to the first chamber. Others **connect** to new chambers.*

    A. move away from
    B. join together
    C. become friends with

6. What does **affect** mean in this book?

*When ants build an anthill, they **affect** the area around them. Sometimes they cause harm.*

    A. cause something to change
    B. make something disappear
    C. leave something behind

Answer key on page 32.

GLOSSARY

bask
To sit or lie in the sun to stay warm.

chamber
A space used as a room.

collapse
To fall down or apart.

dome
A rounded shape that looks like the top half of a ball.

mandibles
Jaws that extend from an ant's head.

mates
Joins together in order to have babies.

nutrients
Substances that humans, animals, and plants need to stay strong and healthy.

queen
A large female ant that lays the eggs for an ant colony.

resources
Things, such as food or water, that animals and plants need to survive.

TO LEARN MORE

BOOKS

Abbott, Henry. *Inside Anthills*. New York: PowerKids Press, 2015.

Ellison, Nora. *Ants Work Together*. New York: PowerKids Press, 2018.

Kenney, Karen Latchana. *Ants*. Minneapolis: Jump!, 2017.

NOTE TO EDUCATORS

Visit **www.focusreaders.com** to find lesson plans, activities, links, and other resources related to this title.

INDEX

Answer Key: 1. Answers will vary; **2.** Answers will vary; **3.** B; **4.** C; **5.** B; **6.** A

32